NATIONAL GEOGRAPHIC

EXPLORE OUR WORLD

WORKBOOK 2

SERIES EDITORS
JoAnn (Jodi) Crandall
Joan Kang Shin

AUTHORS
Jill Florent
Diane Pinkley

CB120985

NATIONAL GEOGRAPHIC LEARNING | CENGAGE Learning

Australia • Brazil • Japan • Korea • Mexico • Singapore • Spain • United Kingdom • United States

Unit 0

1 **Listen and look.** Write. Use words from the box. **TR: 2**

aunt	cousin	dad	grandma	grandpa
me	mom	sister	uncle	

My Family

2 **Read and look.** Write the number.

1. Close your book.
2. Go to the board.
3. Take out your crayons.
4. Hold up your card.
5. Be quiet!
6. Open your book.
7. Work in a group.
8. Raise your hand.
9. Work with a partner.

3 **Listen and write.** Use words from the box. TR: 3

I	our
he	she
her	their
his	they
it	we
its	you
my	your

1.

2.

3.

1. __________ is eating __________ sandwich.

   __________ is eating __________ apple.

2. __________ have __________ crayons.

   __________ have __________ books.

3. __________ am wearing __________ hat.

   __________ are wearing __________ hat.

4. What is the dog wearing?

   __________ is wearing __________ jacket.

4 **Listen and find.** Circle. TR: 4

Unit 1

Animal Friends

1 **Look and match.** Write the number.

☐	a goat	☐	a cow	☐	a chicken
☐	a horse	☐	a cat	☐	a dog
☐	a duck	☐	a turtle	☐	a sheep

GRAMMAR

What **are** the goats **doing?**	They**'re eating.**	**They're** = They are
Are they **running?**	No, they **aren't.**	**aren't** = are not
Are they **walking?**	Yes, they **are.**	

2 **Listen.** Write. TR: 5

1. What ________ the cats doing?
2. What are the horses ________?
3. What are the goats ________?
4. What ________ the cows doing?

3 **Listen.** Write. TR: 6

1. ______________________________
2. ______________________________
3. ______________________________

4 **Look.** Read. Match. Write the numbers.

1. The sheep see a dog.
2. The cat is crawling.
3. The goat is climbing.
4. The ducks are swimming.
5. The ducks are flying.

5 **Listen.** Read. Write. TR: 7

1. I ______________ two turtles.
2. The turtles are ______________.
3. A red bird is ______________.
4. A girl is ______________ a tree.

GRAMMAR

Do you **want to see** the cow?	No, I don't.	don't = do not
Does he **want to see** the cow?	No, he doesn't.	doesn't = does not
What **do** you **want to do**?	I **want to see** the sheep.	
What **does** Ivan **want to do**?	He **wants to ride** the horse.	

6 Listen. Write. TR: 8

1. Do you want to ride a horse?
2. What ______ you ______________________?
3. ______ Lena ______________________ the goats?
4. What ______ she ______________________?

7 Listen and write. Circle. TR: 9

1. ______________________________________? yes no
2. ______________________________________? yes no
3. ______________________________________? yes no

8 **Look and write.** What is different?

1.

2.

1. In 1, the birds are swimming. In 2, they're flying.

2. ____________________

3. ____________________

4. ____________________

5. ____________________

9 **Listen to the song.** Write a new verse. Use words from the box. TR: 10

goats	eating	on the grass
sheep	sleeping	in the sun
ducks	swimming	in the water

I see five ______________________________.

Are they ______________________________?

Yes, they're ______________________________.

They're ______________________________.

10 **Listen.** Which words have the sound of **d** as in **d**og? Color the stars. TR: 11

11 **Listen and read.** TR: 12

More Baby Animals

A baby turtle comes from an egg. Do you see the egg?

Let's learn about more baby animals. A baby cow is called a calf. A baby horse is a foal. A baby goat is a kid. A baby turtle is called a hatchling. There are many baby animals!

12 **Read and write.**

What are your favorite baby animals? ______________________

____

____

13 **Read.**

My favorite animal is my cat. Her name is Missy. She is white, brown, and gray. Missy has two kittens. They are so cute! Boots is black with two white feet. Snowy is all white. I love them all.

14 **Draw and write about your favorite animal.**

My favorite animal is ______________________________

____

____

____

______________________________.

Unit 2

Fun in Class

1 Look and match. Write the number.

[ ] coloring [ ] counting [ ] cutting [ ] drawing

[ ] erasing [ ] gluing [ ] talking

GRAMMAR

What **are** you **doing**? We'**re erasing** the board. | **we're** = we + are

2 **Look and listen.** Write numbers. TR: 13

☐ 

☐ 

☐ 

☐ 

3 **Listen again.** Write sentences. TR: 14

1. ______________________
2. ______________________
3. ______________________
4. ______________________

4 **Look and read.** Write a sentence.

coloring cooking reading watching TV

What are you doing?

1. We're ______________________

What are you doing?

2. ______________________

5 **Match.** Draw lines.

glue

a marker

a notebook

a paintbrush

scissors

6 **Listen.** What do the students have? Write. **TR: 15**

1. a paintbrush ____________
2. ____________
3. ____________
4. ____________
5. ____________

GRAMMAR

Are there any pencils? Yes, **there are.**

Are there any pens? No, **there aren't.**

aren't = are + not

7 Look, read, and write.

1. Are there any notebooks?

____

2. Are there any markers?

____

3. Are there any erasers?

____

4. Are there any scissors?

____

8 Look and write.

Look at the picture in Activity 7. Write questions. Use the words in the box.

crayons paintbrushes

1. _______________ ? Yes, there are.

2. _______________ ? No, there aren't.

9 **Look.** Read and write.

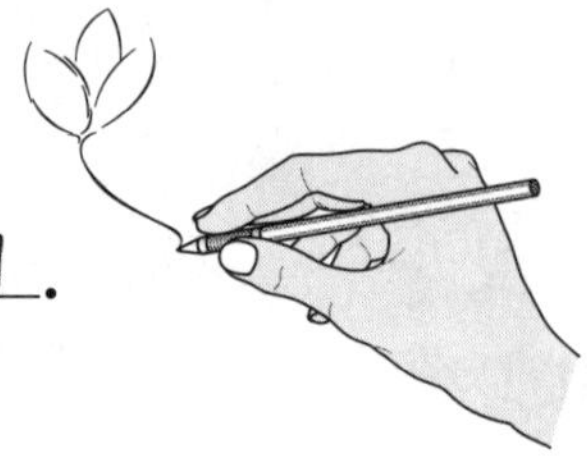

1. I am d r a [w] i n g.

2. I am ☆ __ __ __ __ __ __.

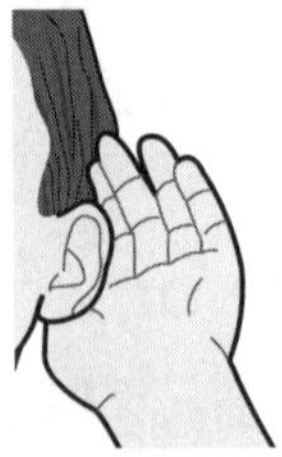

3. I am __ ○ __ __ __ __ __ __ __.

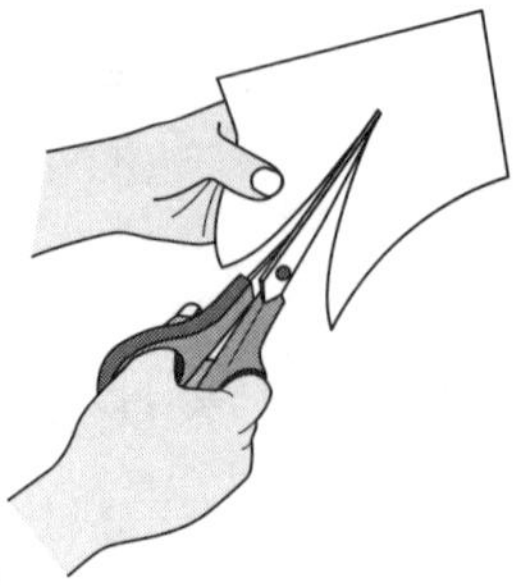

4. I am __ __ __ □ __ __ __.

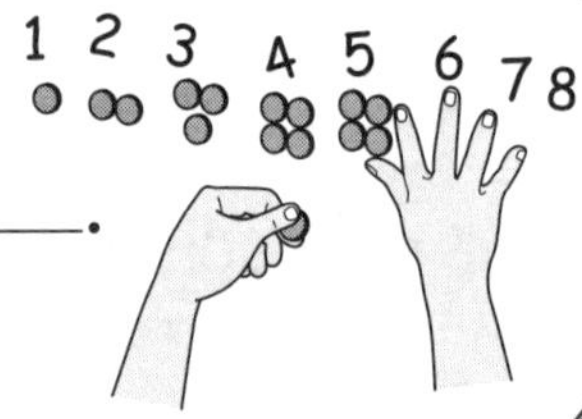

5. I am __ __ __ ◇ __ __ __ __.

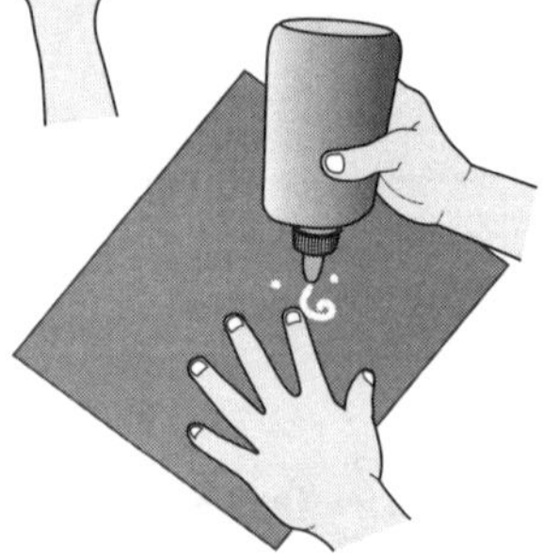

6. I am △ __ __ __ __ __.

10 **Read and answer.** Use the code.

What are *you* doing?

I am □ ☆ ○ □ ○ ◇ △!

11 **Listen and read.** Can you say these fast? TR: 16

1. Sally's sister uses small silver scissors.
2. Green glue is on Grandmother's green gloves.
3. People paint purple paper puppets.

12 **Listen to the song.** Read and circle *yes* or *no*. **TR: 17**

1. We're cutting, We're gluing. yes no
2. We're cutting. We're drawing. yes no
3. We're coloring pictures. yes no
4. We're talking. We're walking. yes no
5. We're talking. We're writing. yes no
6. We're listening to our teacher. yes no

13 **Listen and write.** Listen to words that have the **c** sound in **c**at. Write the words in the crossword puzzle. **TR: 18**

ACROSS

1. 

5. 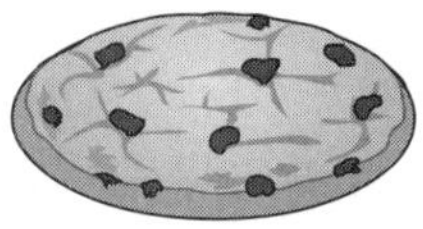

6. 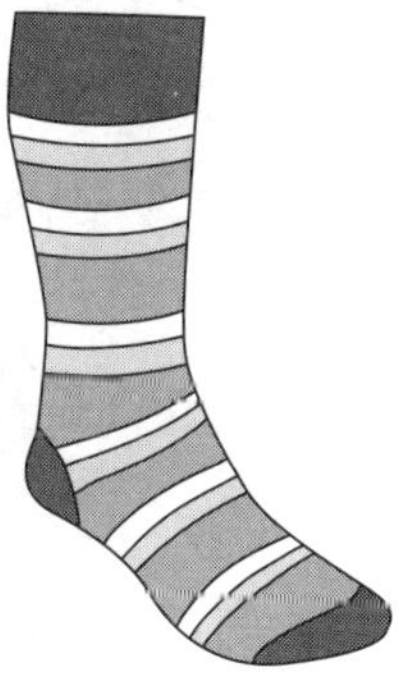

7. 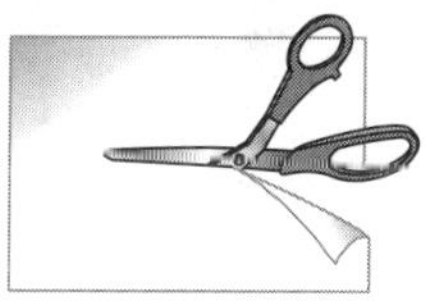

8. 

DOWN

2. 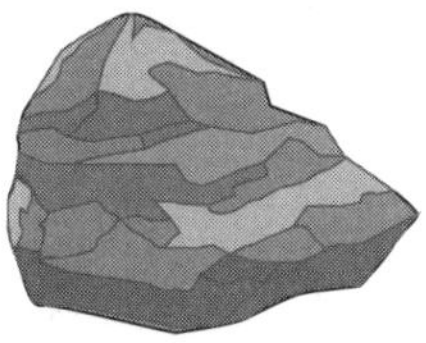

3. 

4. 

14 **Listen and read.** TR: 19

Mexican Yarn Paintings

This Mexican artist is making a picture. But he is not using a paintbrush! He is using beeswax and yarn. He is pressing yarn into the beeswax.

You can make a yarn painting, too. Cut yarn. Glue it to paper.

15 **Choose the right answer.** Circle.

1. The Mexican artist uses	**beeswax and yarn.**	**crayons and glue.**
2. You can use	**paint.**	**glue.**

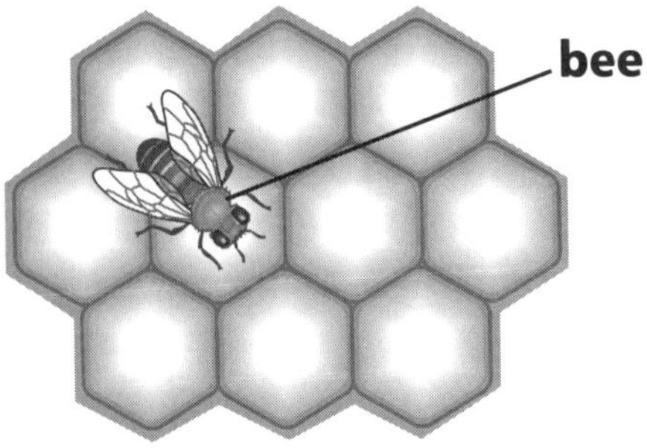

Bees make their homes from beeswax. Each room is the same. Each room has six sides!

16 **Read.**

This is a picture of Sami and me. We are making a big robot. Sami is cutting shapes. I am gluing paper.

17 **Draw and write.** Draw a picture of you and your friend.

1. Who is in the picture?

____

2. What are you making?

____

3. What are you doing?

____

18 **Write.** Put your sentences from Activity 17 together.

This is a picture of _______________________________

____

____

____

____.

Unit 3

Boots and Bathing Suits

1 **Look.** Write numbers and words.

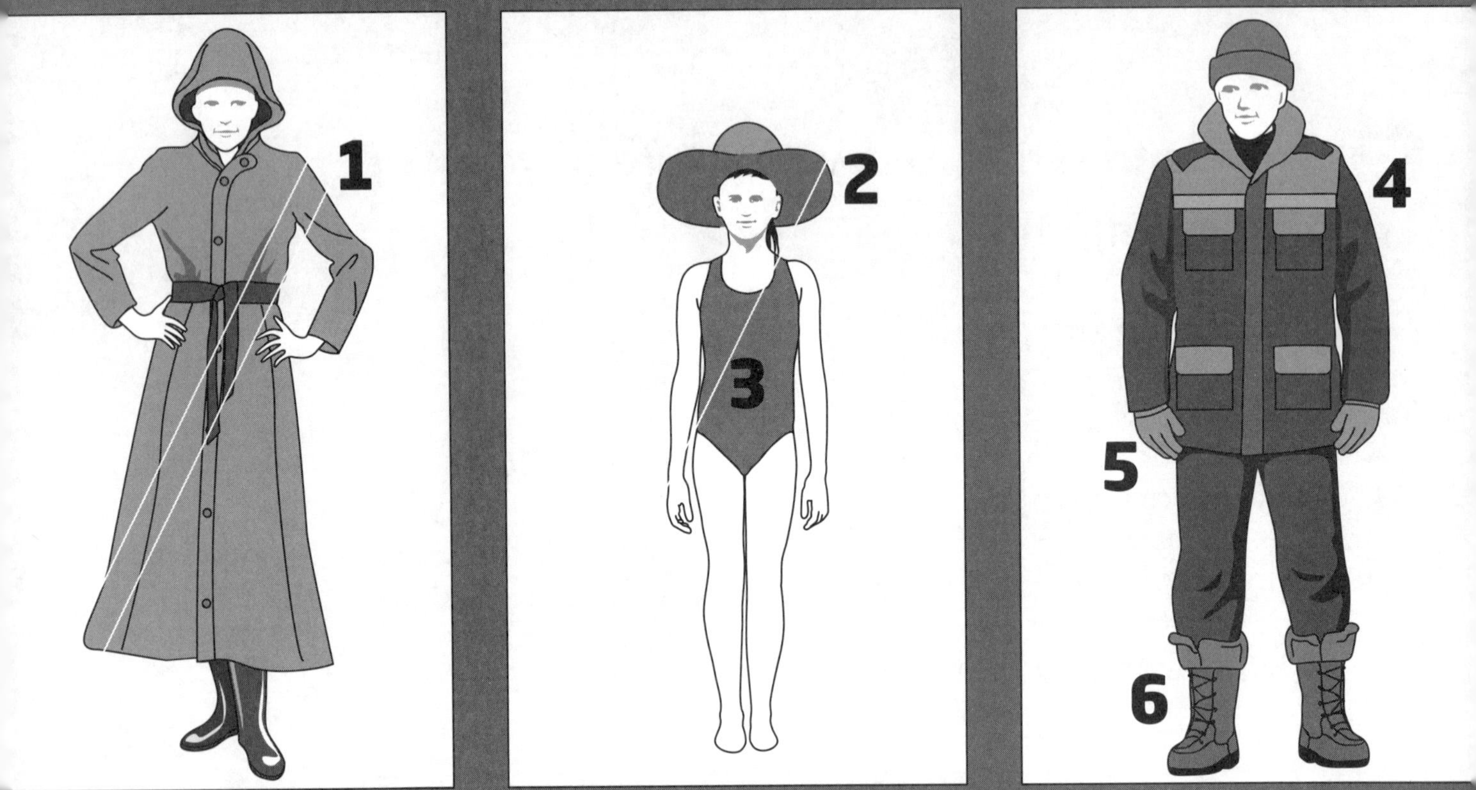

☐ bathing suit ☐ boots ☐ gloves

☐ hat ☐ jacket ☐ raincoat

cloudy cold hot rainy sunny

1. Wear a raincoat in __________ and __________ weather.
2. Wear a bathing suit in __________ and __________ weather.
3. Wear gloves in __________ weather.

GRAMMAR

What day **is it?**	**It's** Friday.	**it's** = it + is
What's the weather **like?**	**It's** rainy.	**what's** = what + is

2 Listen, read, and write. TR: 20

1. It's Monday. What's the weather like? It's ____________.
2. It's Tuesday. What's the weather like? It's ____________.
3. It's Wednesday. What's the weather like? It's ____________.

1.

rainy

2.

cold

3.

sunny

3 **Can it be true?** Check **T** for *True* and **F** for *False*.

1. It's sunny and rainy.	(T)	(F)
2. It's cold and hot.	(T)	(F)
3. It's sunny and cold.	(T)	(F)
4. It's cloudy and rainy.	(T)	(F)

4 Write about the weather.

____

____

5 **Listen.** Write. TR: 21

a coat | jeans | shorts | sneakers | an umbrella

1. It's an umbrella.
2. They're ________.
3. They're ________.
4. It's ________.
5. They're ________.

6 **What's missing?** Write. Use the words in the boxes.

1.

boots gloves sneakers

2.

socks shoes umbrella

3.

coat skirt shorts

GRAMMAR

It's cold.	**Put on** your gloves.	it's = it + is
It's hot.	**Take off** your jacket.	
It's cloudy.	**Don't forget** your umbrella.	don't = do + not

7 Read and write.

1. It's hot. ________________ your boots.
2. It's cold. ________________ your jacket.
3. It's sunny. ________________ your raincoat.
4. It's rainy. ________________ your umbrella.

8 Look and write.

forget / your boots	put on / your jacket
take off / my hat	take off / my shoes

1. Take off my hat.

________________.

2. ________________

________________.

3. ________________

________________.

4. ________________

________________.

9 **Read.** Do the puzzles.

1. What's the weather like?

   It's not raining. It's sunny.

   Take off your ________ (across) and boots.

   Put on your ________ (down).

2. What's the weather like?

   It's ________ (down).

   and ________ (across).

   Don't forget your coat and hat.

   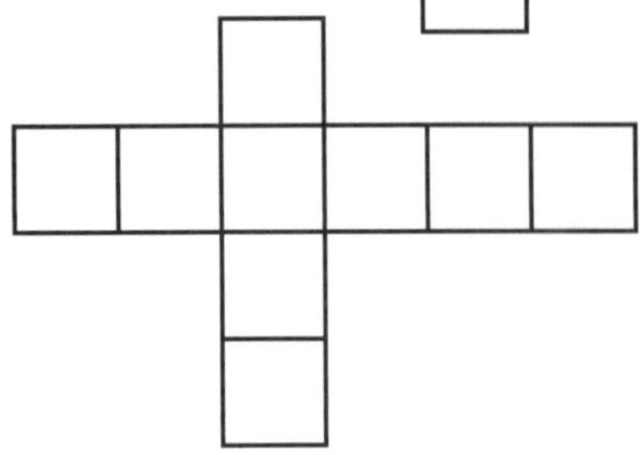

3. What's the weather like?

   It's sunny.

   Put on your ________ (down)

   and ________ (across).

   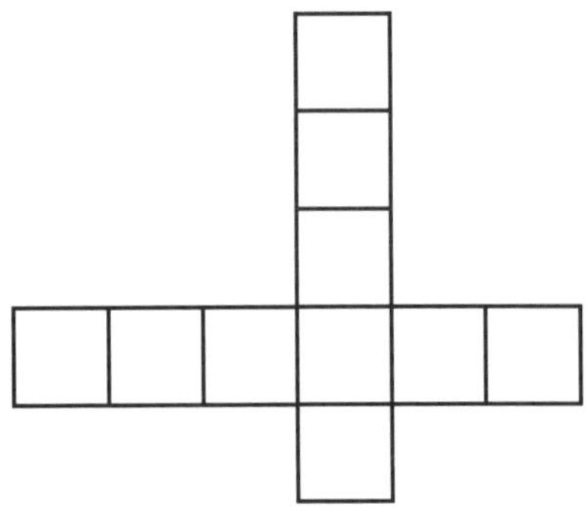

10 **Listen and read.** Can you say these fast? TR: 22

1. We have wet, windy, Wednesday weather!
2. What color coat can Cousin Carlos get?
3. Suzu's sister Sada likes socks, shoes, and shorts.

11 **Listen to the song.** Read and write. TR: 23

raincoat and pants	boots and coat
sneakers and shorts	shirt and gloves

Today it's snowy.

Put on your

________________________.

It's cold outside today.

Today it's sunny.

Put on your

________________________.

It's hot outside today.

12 **Listen.** Draw an X over the word that doesn't have the same **r** sound as in **r**ainy. TR: 24

1.

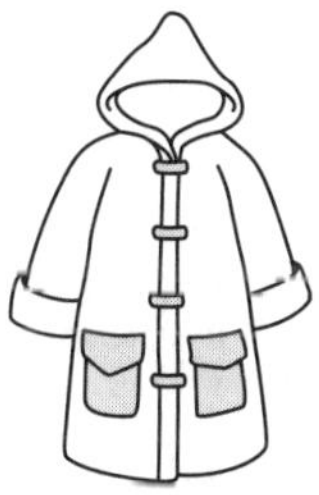

2.

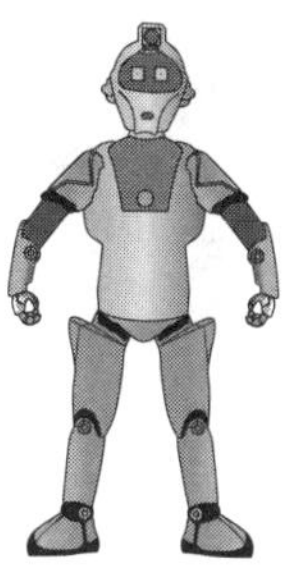

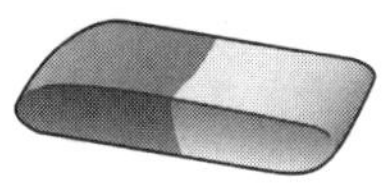

3.

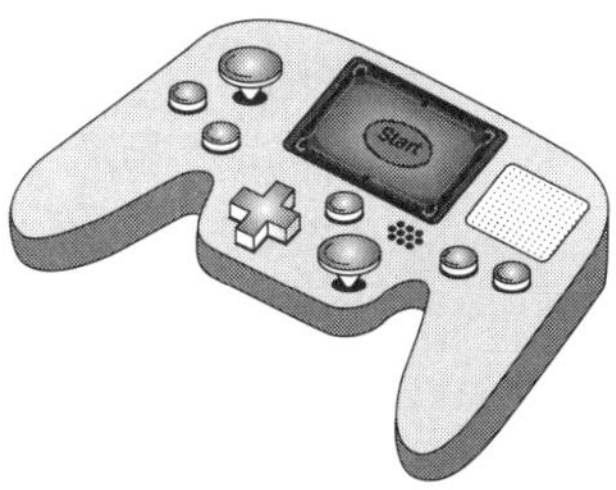

13 Listen and read. TR: 25

Hats

People wear many kinds of hats. A hat keeps you warm on a cold day. You can wear a hat on a hot day. Or you can wear a hat when it's rainy. You can even wear a hat just for fun!

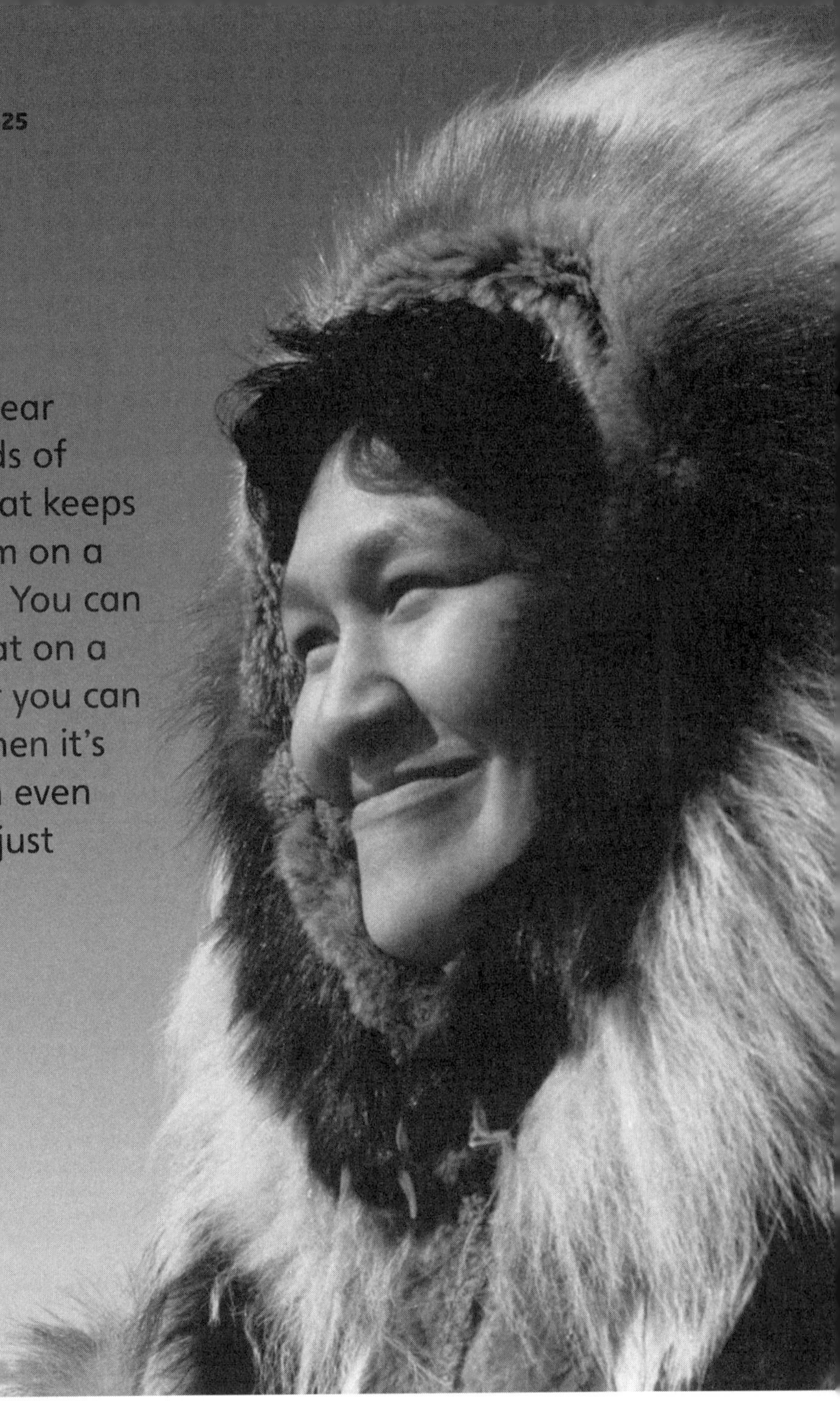

14 Write. Write about your favorite hat.

1. What color is your hat? ______________________

2. When do you wear your hat? ______________________

15 **Read.**

In this photo, I'm with my friends. We're having fun. It's a hot and sunny day. I'm wearing a shirt, shorts, and a sun hat. Do you see me?

16 **Write.** What about you? Use a picture of yourself.

1. Where are you? Who are you with?

____

2. What is the weather like?

____

3. What are you wearing?

____

17 **Write.** Put your sentences from Activity 16 together.

In this photo, I ____

____

____

____

____.

Unit 4

Fun in the Sun

1 Look and write.

fly a kite
jump rope
play a game
play baseball
play basketball
play soccer
ride a bike

____

____

____

____

2 **Write.** What do you want to do?

 I want to jump rope.

 ______________________

 ______________________

GRAMMAR

Do you **like to play** soccer?	Yes, I do. It's fun.	it's = it + is
Do you **like to fly** a kite?	No, I don't. It's boring.	don't = do not
What do you **like to do**?	I **like to play** soccer.	
What do they **like to do**?	They **like to ride a bike.**	

3 **Look and listen.** Write numbers. **TR: 26**

4 **Write.** Make two lists.

I like to...	I don't like to...
	I don't like to play baseball.

5 **Listen and write.** Number the pictures. **TR: 27**

1

6 **What do you like to do?** Write **it's fun** if you like it. Write **it's boring** if you don't like it.

bounce a ball	
catch a ball	
play tag	
throw a ball	
watch a game	

7 **Write about your chart.**

1. I ____________________________. It's ________________.

2. I don't ____________________________. It's ________________.

GRAMMAR

Let's watch a game. OK. What fun!

Let's play tag. No, thanks.

let's = let us

8 Read and write.

Let's throw a ball. ______ bounce a ball. ______ fly a kite.

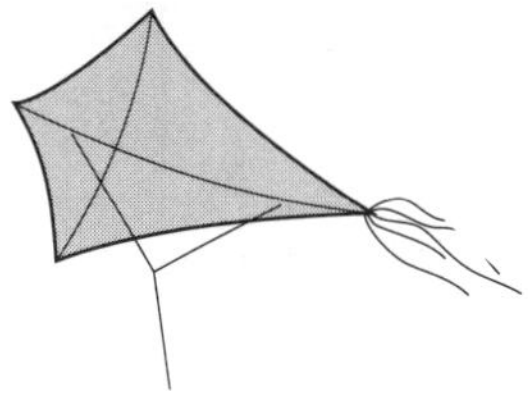

______ play soccer. ______ jump rope. ______ catch a ball.

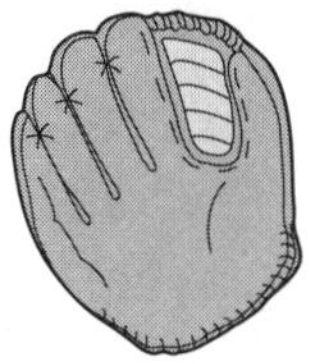

9 Draw and write. What do you want to do?

1. Let's play soccer. OK. No, thanks.
2. ______ play basketball. ______
3. ______ watch a game. ______
4. ______ play tag. ______

10 **Listen and draw.** Draw a line from START to END. TR: 28

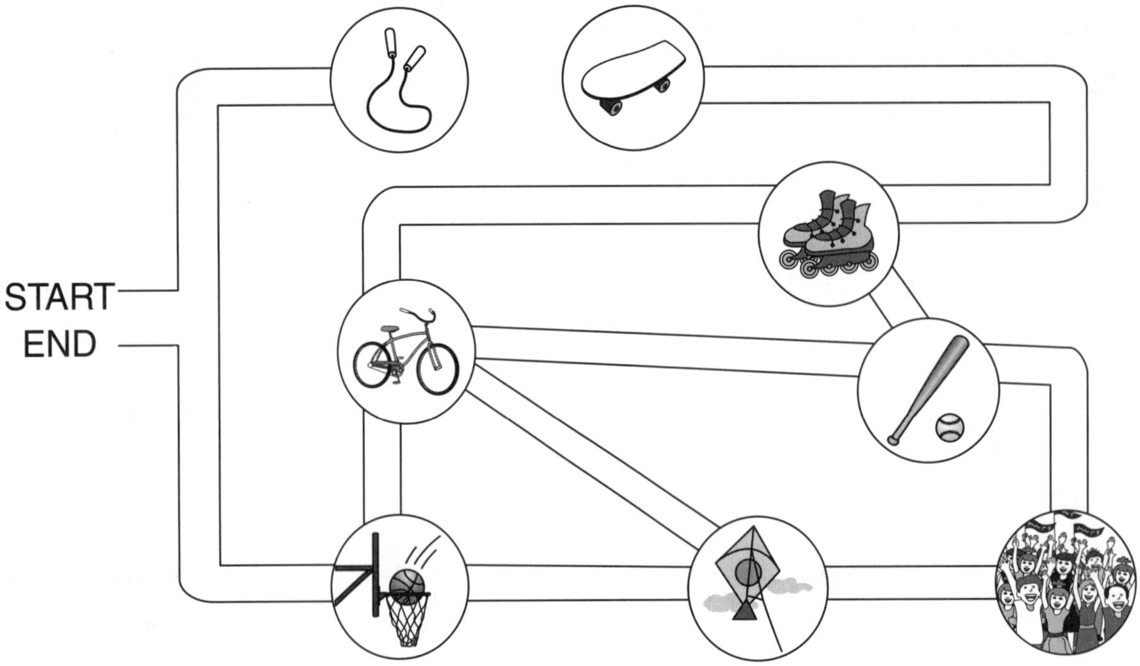

11 **Look.** Choose. Write what you like ☺.

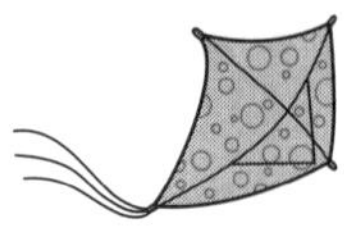 OR 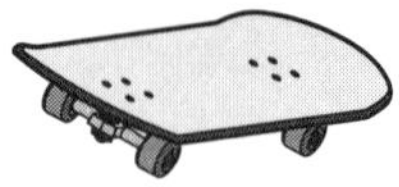

☺ Let's fly a kite.

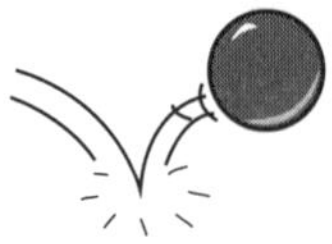 OR 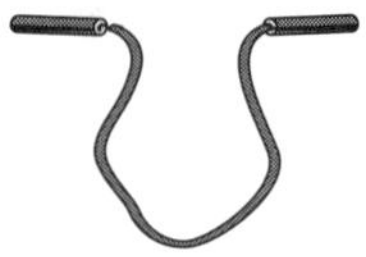

☺ ____________________

 OR 

☺ ____________________

12 **Listen and read.** Can you say these fast? TR: 29

1. Big boys bounce brown basketballs.
2. Six silly soccer stars sing sad songs.

13 **Listen to the song.** Draw lines. TR: 30

1. I like to  .

   Yes, I do. Yes, I do.

2. I like to 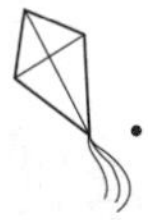 .

   Yes, I do. Yes, I do.

3. I like to 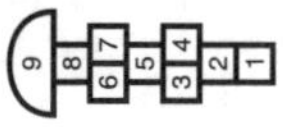 .

   I like to play outside with you.

4. I like to  .

   Yes, I do. Yes, I do.

5. I like to  .

   I like to play with you.

climb a tree
play games
swim
ride a bike
play basketball
play baseball
fly a kite
jump rope
play soccer

14 **Listen.** Which words have a sound like the **u** in s**u**n? Draw a line to connect the pictures. TR: 31

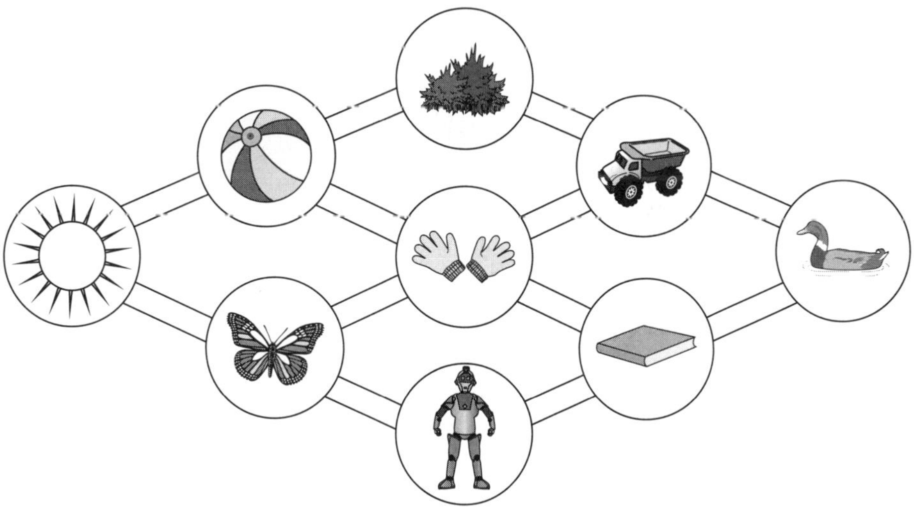

15 **Say the words.** How many times do you hear **u** as in s**u**n? Write. ☐

blue	cut	jump	paintbrush
puzzle	run	turtle	umbrella

16 Listen and read. TR: 32

The X Games

skateboard

ski

snowboard

People all around the world like to watch the X Games. The X Games take place in hot weather and cold weather.

Hot Weather The players like to skateboard and ride bikes. The players like to go fast.

Cold Weather The players like the snow. They ski and snowboard. They go fast.

Do you like to watch TV? Watch the X Games!

17 Read. Check T for *True* and F for *False*.

1. They play the X Games only in hot weather. Ⓣ Ⓕ
2. In hot weather, they ride bikes. Ⓣ Ⓕ
3. Players skateboard in cold weather. Ⓣ Ⓕ

18 You are in the X Games!

Draw and write.

I am in the X Games.

The weather is ____________.

I like ______________________

______________________.

19 **Read.**

At home I like to ride my bike. At school I like to play tag. It's fun. On Saturday I like to play basketball with my friends.

20 **Write.** Write about what you like to do.

1. What do you like to do at home?

____

2. What do you like to do at school?

____

3. What do you like to do on Saturday?

____

21 **Write.** Put your sentences from Activity 20 together.

____

____

____

____

______________________________.

Review

1 **Look.** Read. Underline the correct answer.

1. What are they doing?

   They're swimming.

   They're walking.

2. What are they doing?

   They're flying.

   They're climbing.

3. What are they doing?

   They're eating.

   They're sleeping.

4. What are you doing?

   We're counting.

   We're talking.

5. What are you doing?

   We're drawing.

   We're writing.

6. What are you doing?

   I'm gluing paper.

   I'm cutting paper.

2 **Read.** Look at page 36. Write.

1. Are there any boots? No, there aren't.
2. Are there any scissors? ______________
3. Are there any sheep? ______________
4. Are there any goats? ______________

3 **What's the weather like?** Read. Underline the correct answer.

1. 

It's **sunny. / rainy.**

Take off / Put on your raincoat.

Don't forget your **shorts. / umbrella.**

2. 

It's **cloudy. / sunny.**

Take off / Put on your jacket.

Put on your **bathing suit. / coat.**

4 **Listen.** Read. Match. Draw a line. **TR: 33**

1. Do you like to play baseball?	a. I like to play tag.
2. What do they like to do?	b. OK. What fun!
3. Do you like to bounce a ball?	c. They like to ride horses.
4. What do you like to do?	d. Yes, I do. It's fun.
5. Let's glue stars on our notebooks.	e. No, I don't. It's boring.
6. It's cloudy.	f. Let's take umbrellas.

Unit 5

Inside Our House

1 Look and write.

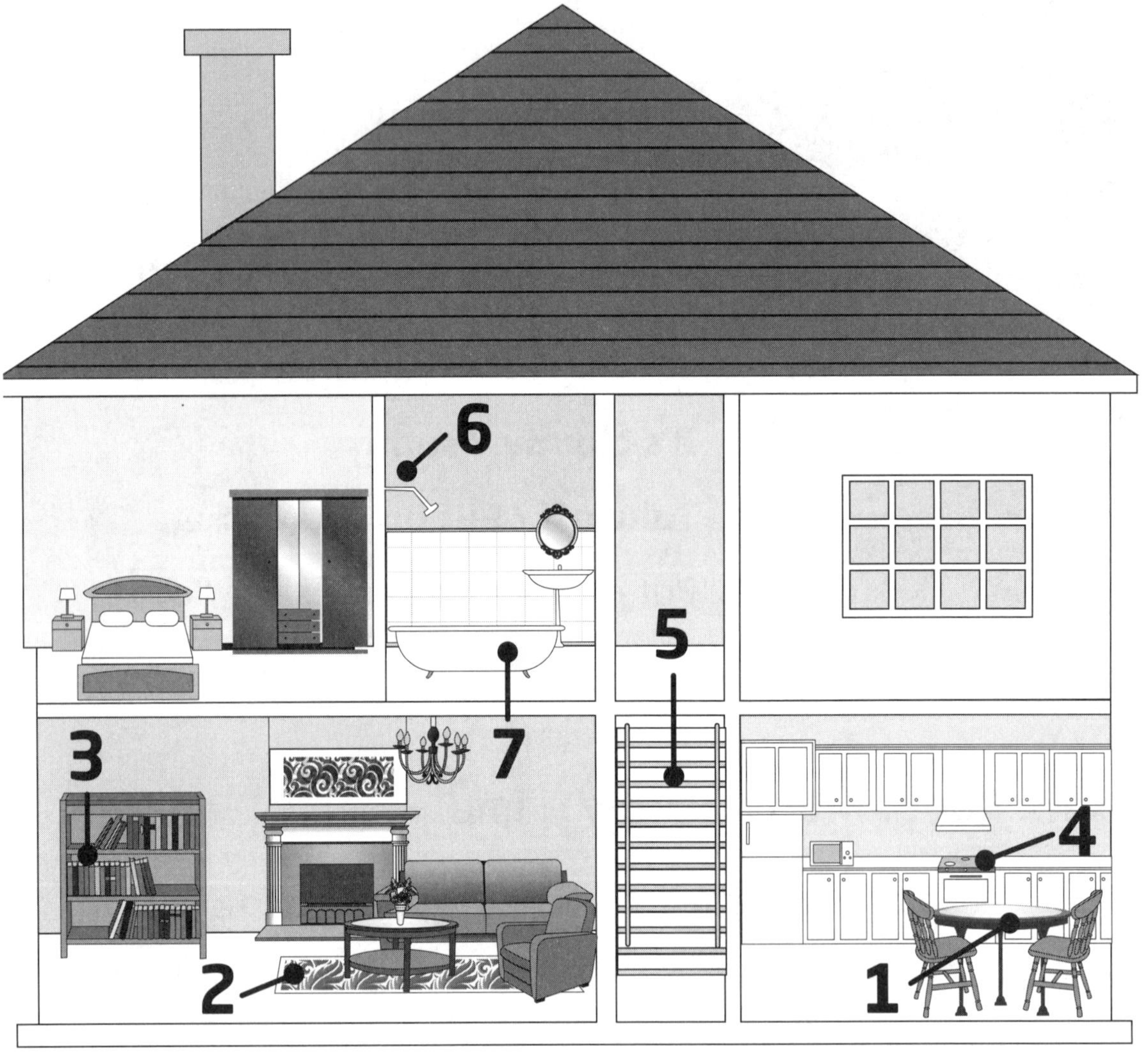

☐ a bookcase	☐ a rug	☐ a shower	☐ stairs
☐ a stove	☐ a table	☐ a tub	

GRAMMAR

Where is the ● ?

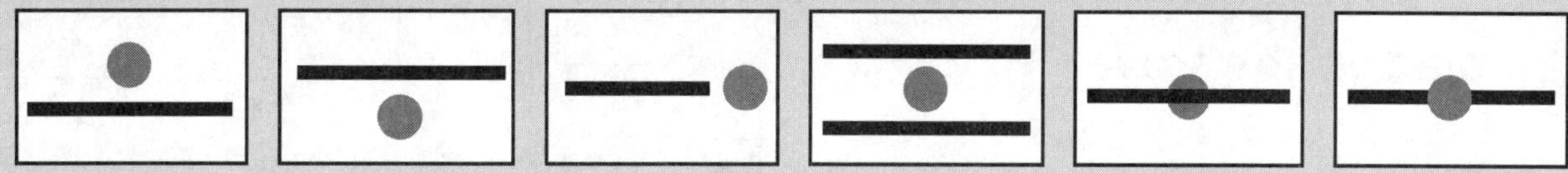

above **under** **next to** **between** **behind** **in front of**

2 Look and write.

1. The shelf is ________________ the desk.
2. The scissors are ________________ the paper.
3. The pencils are ________________ the paper and the notebook.
4. The notebook is ________________ the glue.
5. The picture is ________________ the notebook.
6. The glue is ________________ the notebook.

3 Listen and do. TR: 34

4 **Read and match.** Draw lines.

1. The refrigerator is next to the stove.
2. The window is next to the stove.
3. The stove is next to the sink.
4. The phone is next to the stove.
5. The stove is next to the door.

A

B
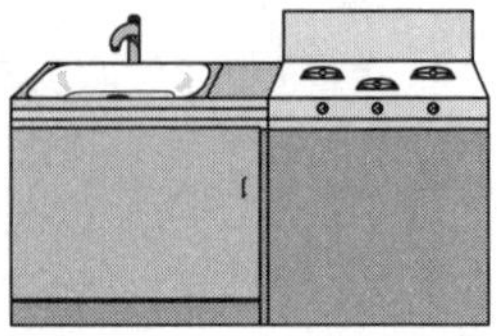

C
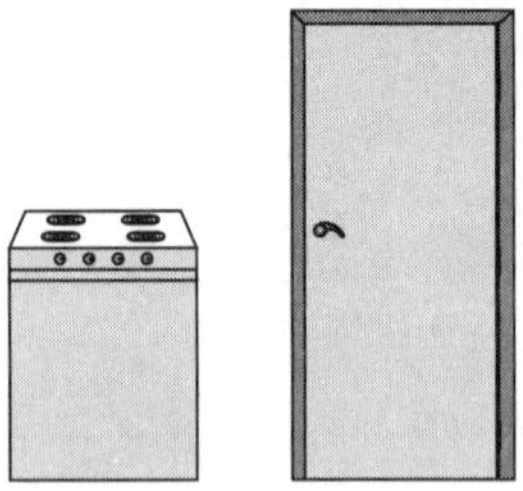

D

E
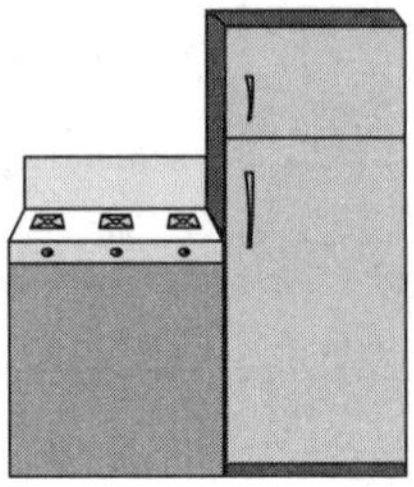

5 **Look and write.**

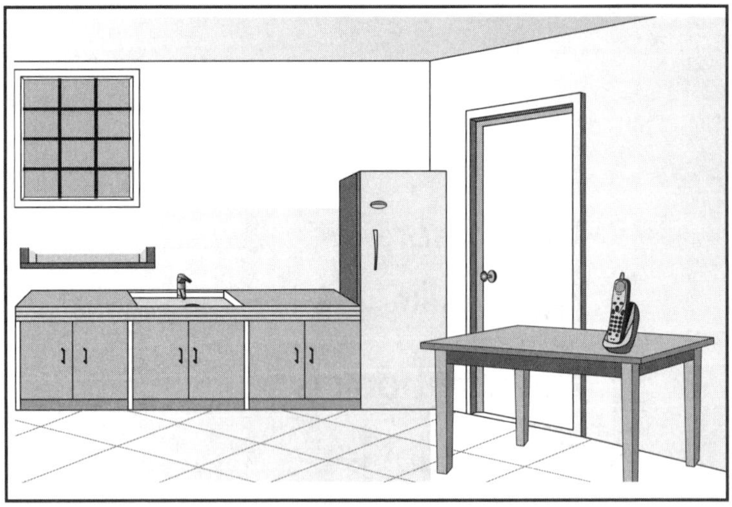

1. There is a ______________ above the shelf.
2. The ______________ is between the shelf and the refrigerator.
3. The ______________ is on the table.
4. There is a ______________ between the sink and the door.

GRAMMAR

Where is the **picture**?	**It's** above the desk.	**It's** = It is
Where are the **boots**?	**They're** under the bed.	**They're** = They are

6 Listen and answer. TR: 35

1. ________ in front of the sofa.
2. ________ next to the fireplace.
3. ________ between the chairs.
4. ________ above the fireplace.

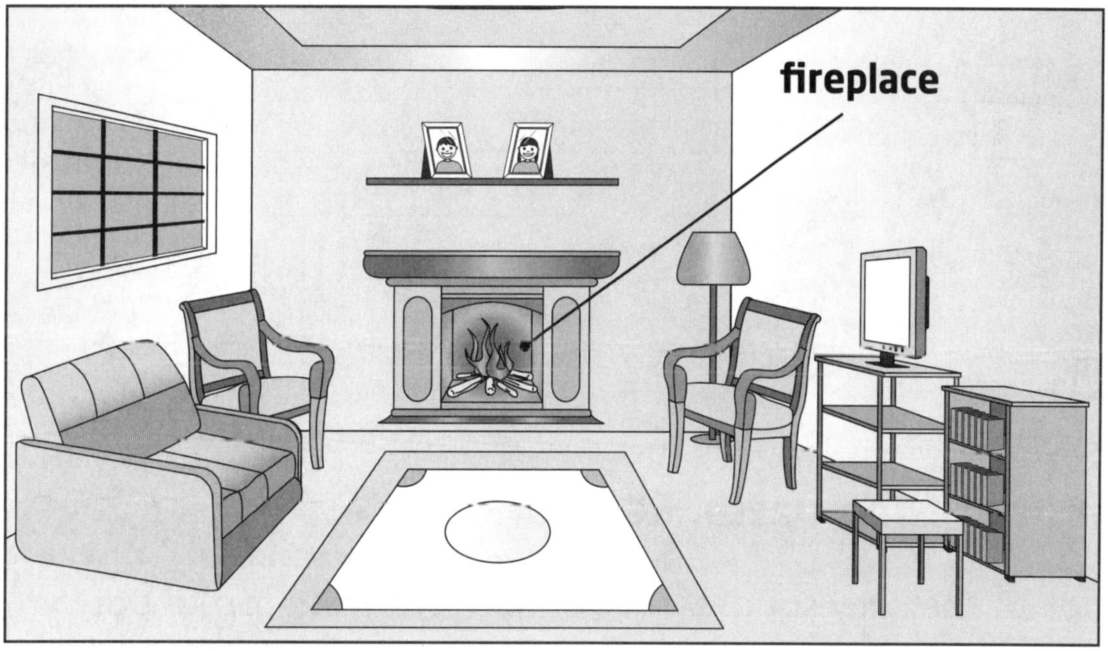

7 **Look at the picture.** Read and write.

1. Where is the lamp?
   It's ________ behind a chair.
2. Where is the window?
   ________ above the sofa.
3. Where is the rug?
   ________ in front of the fireplace.
4. Where are the pictures?
   ________ on the shelf.

8 Do the puzzle.

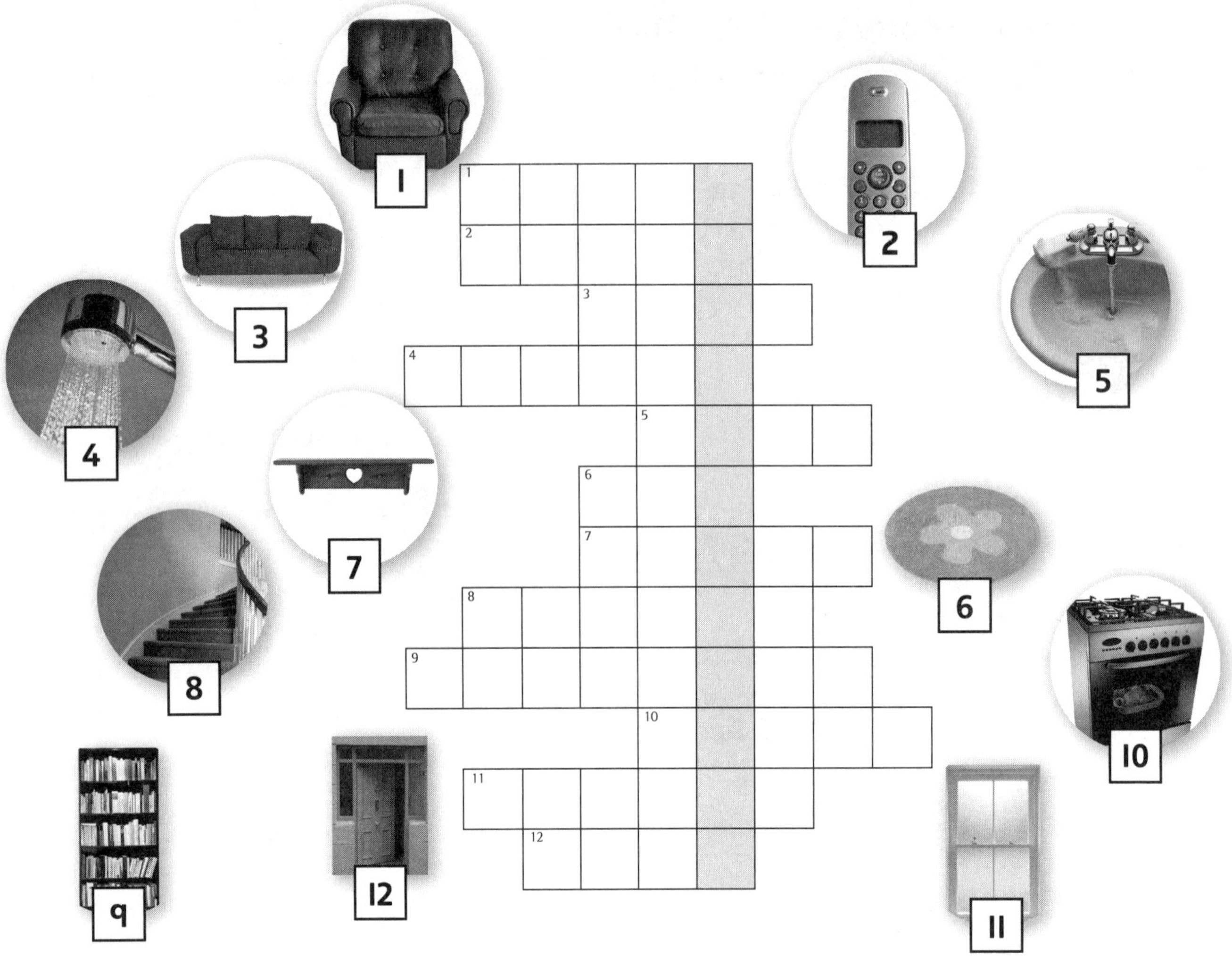

9 **Look at the puzzle.** Read and write.

Look at the *gray* squares. Read the word from top to bottom.

What is the word? ________________ Where is it? In the____________.

10 **Listen and read.** Can you say these fast? **TR: 36**

1. There isn't a shelf in the shower.
2. Take the stove up the stairs.
3. Next to the window, behind the door, under the table, above the floor.

11 **Listen to the song.** Write a new verse. Use some words from the box. **TR: 37**

chair	bathroom	bed	bedroom	bookcase	lamp	living room
rug	shower	sink	sofa	tub	TV	

Where is the ____________________? It's in the ____________________.

Where is the ____________________? It's in the ____________________.

Where is the ____________________? It's in the ____________________.

12 **Listen.** Which words have **a** that sounds like the **a** in table? Check the boxes. **TR: 38**

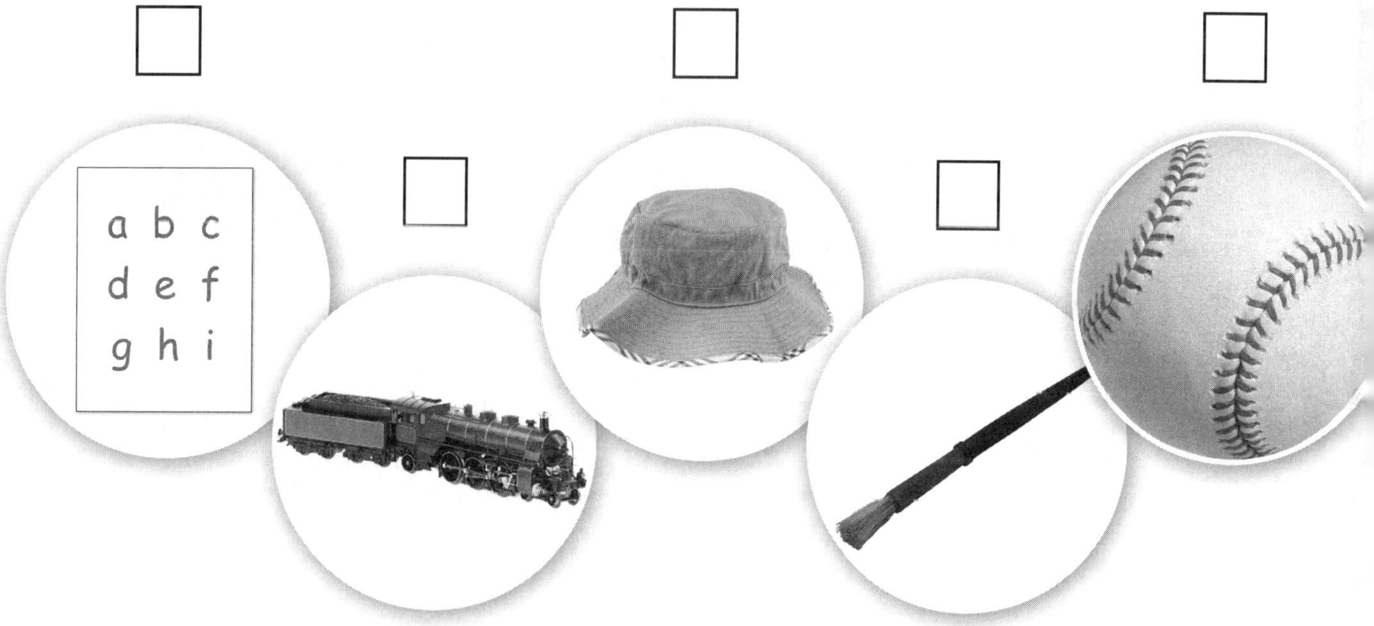

13 **Say the words.** How many times do you hear **a** as in table? Write. ☐

basketball	bookcase	crayon	eraser
game	lemonade	raincoat	stairs

14 Listen and read. TR: 39

Welcome to My Home

An Apartment

Alice and her family live in an apartment. The apartment is in a big building. There is a living room with a big sofa and a TV. The kitchen is between the living room and Alice's bedroom. Alice and her sister share a bedroom. Her parents' bedroom is next to the bathroom.

an apartment

A Mobile Home

Ben's family lives in a mobile home in the summer. There's a table and four chairs in the living room. There's a stove, a sink, and a refrigerator in the kitchen. There is a bathroom with a shower. Ben's parents drive the mobile home to new places. They have lots of fun!

mobile homes

15 Read and write.

1. How many bedrooms are in Alice's apartment?

   ____

2. Can Ben's parents drive the mobile home? ______________
3. Is the apartment in a building? ______________
4. Is the mobile home in a building? ______________

16 Read.

This is my living room. It's my favorite room. There is a big rug in front of the fireplace. I like to do my puzzles there. There is an armchair next to the sofa. I like to sit on the sofa and watch TV.

17 Write. Write about a room in your house.

1. What room are you writing about?

____

2. Describe the room and furniture.

____

____

3. What do you like to do in the room?

____

18 Write. Put your sentences from Activity 17 together.

This is my _______________________________________

____

____

____.

Unit 6

Day by Day

1 **Look and match.** Write the number.

1 

2 

3 

4 

5 

6 

7 

8 

9 

☐ I get up.
☐ I play with friends.
☐ I eat breakfast.
☐ I eat lunch.
☐ I get dressed.
☐ I go to school.
☐ I go to bed.
☐ I eat dinner.
☐ I brush my teeth.

GRAMMAR

What time is it?	**It's** 4:00.	It's four **o'clock**.
When do you go to school?	**At** 8:00.	At eight **o'clock**.
When does she eat dinner?	**At** 6:00.	At six **o'clock**.

2 **Read, look, and match.** Draw lines.

1. It's one o'clock.

2. It's seven o'clock.

3. It's five o'clock.

4. It's twelve o'clock.

5. It's nine o'clock.

3 **Read and write.** Choose a word from the box.

at it's

1. I get up _____ seven o'clock.
2. _____ one o'clock. I'm eating lunch.
3. I go to school _____ eight o'clock.
4. _____ nine o'clock. I'm going to bed.

4 **Read and look.** Match. Draw lines.

1. We go to bed at night.

2. We go to school in the morning.

3. We watch TV in the evening.

4. We play in the park in the afternoon.

5 **Read and guess.** Write. Use words from the box.

at night   in the afternoon   in the evening   in the morning

1. I am with my friends. We are walking home from school.

____

2. I look out my window. It's sunny. I'm putting on my red shirt and blue jeans.

____

3. I'm on the sofa with my family. We are watching our favorite TV show.

____

GRAMMAR

What do you do **every day**? I **always** take a bath.

What does your sister do in the morning?

She reads. She **never** watches TV in the morning.

6 **Read and match.** Write. What do you always do? What do you never do?

I	always never	go play eat	lunch to school to bed breakfast with friends games	in the morning. in the afternoon. in the evening. at night.

1. I never go to bed in the morning.
2. ______________________
3. ______________________
4. ______________________

7 **Draw and write.** What do you do every day?

I ______________________

____

____

every day.

8 **Listen and draw lines.** TR: 40

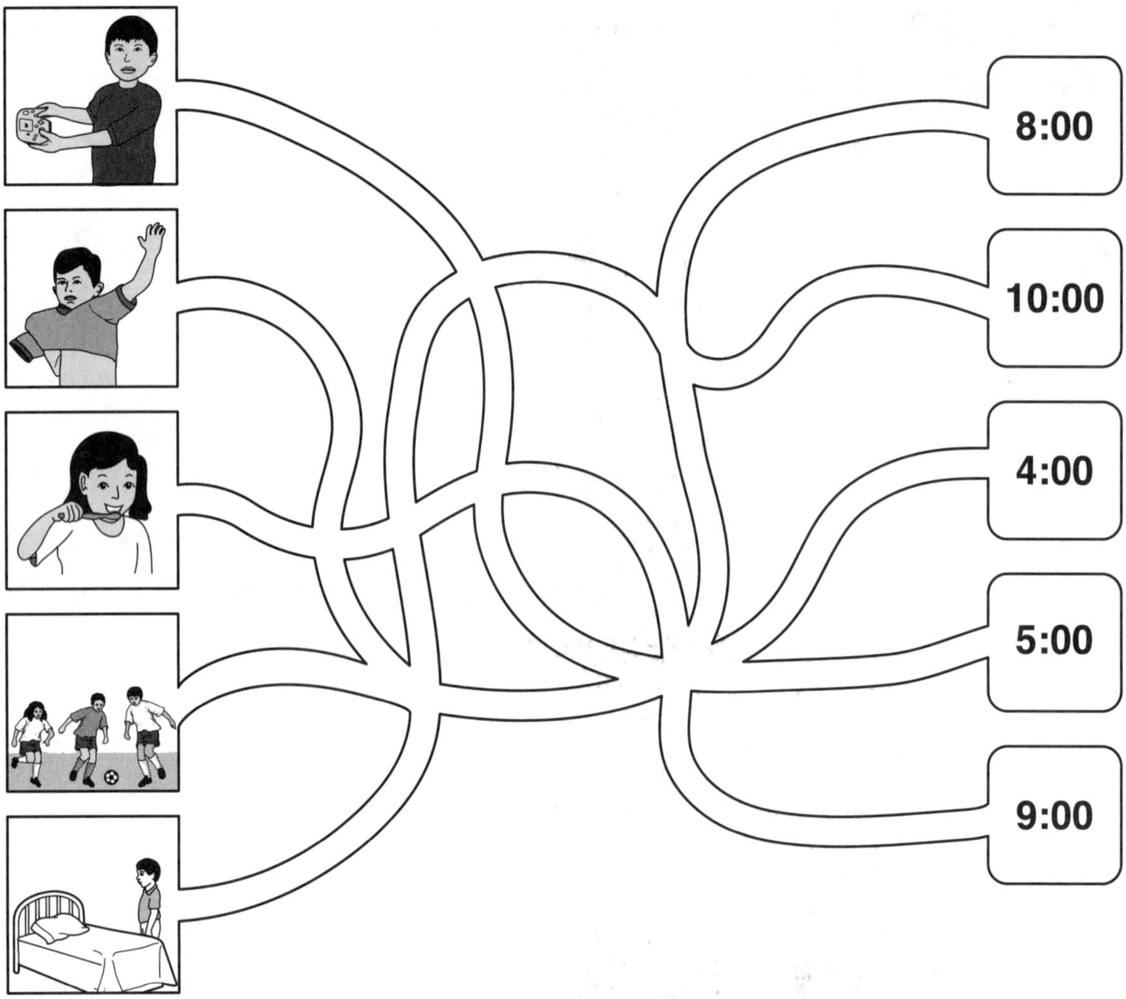

9 **What do you always do?** Unscramble and write.

I wasyal rewit ni ym borkokow.

____

10 **Listen and read.** Can you say these fast? TR: 41

1. We always play in the park.
2. Never bounce a ball in the bathroom.
3. Eat an apple every night at eight o'clock.

11 **Listen to the song.** Write a new verse. Use some words from the box. TR: 42

one	get dressed	afternoon
four	play a game	evening
five	read my book	morning
six	ride my bike	
eleven	take a bath	

It's ______________ o'clock. It's ______________ o'clock.

It's ______________ o'clock in the ______________.

I always ______________ at ______________ every day.

I ______________ at ______________ every day.

12 **Listen.** Which words have **g** that sounds like the **g** in **g**o? Color. TR: 43

1. 

2. 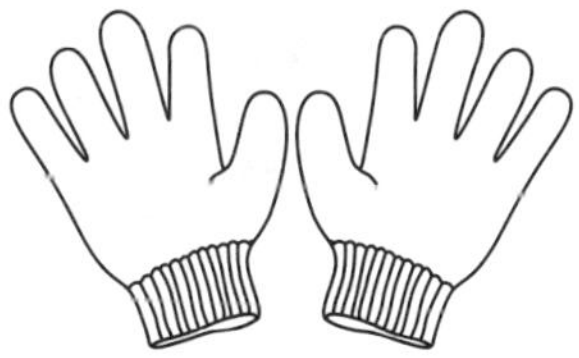

3. 

4. 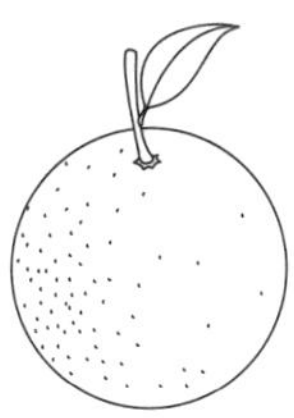

5. 

13 **Say the words.** How many times do you hear **g** as in **g**o? Write. ☐

big	get	glue	grandfather
green	play tag	refrigerator	triangle

14 Listen and read. TR: 44

Tubby the Labrador

Dog Helps Planet

This is Tubby. He's a smart dog! Every day he goes to the park for a walk. Tubby never plays with a ball. He picks up many plastic bottles every day. Tubby helps to keep the park clean. This is how he helps the planet. Do you help to keep the planet clean, too?

15 **Read.** Check **T** for *True* and **F** for *False*.

1. Tubby goes to the park every day. Ⓣ Ⓕ
2. Tubby likes to play with a ball. Ⓣ Ⓕ
3. Tubby likes to pick up plastic bottles. Ⓣ Ⓕ

16 **Read.**

My favorite day is Saturday. I never eat breakfast before 10 o'clock in the morning. I ride my bike or rollerblade with my friends in the afternoon. I play video games with my sister in the evening. Saturday is always a great day!

17 **Write.** Write about your favorite day.

1. What is your favorite day?

____

2. What do you do in the morning?

____

3. What do you do in the afternoon?

____

4. What do you do in the evening?

____

18 **Write.** Put your sentences from Activity 17 together.

My favorite day is ____

____

____

____

____.

Unit 7

How Are You?

1 Look and write.

1

2

3

4

5

6

7

8

9

☐ surprised ☐ tired ☐ happy ☐ angry ☐ thirsty

☐ scared ☐ sad ☐ bored ☐ hungry

GRAMMAR

How are you?	I'm **OK.** I'm **fine.**	I'm **great!** We're **great!**
You **look** tired.	Yes. I'm tired.	No. We're bored.
She **looks** scared. He **looks** tired. They **look** angry.	No. She's surprised. Yes. He's tired. No. They're bored.	

2 Listen and write. TR: 45

1. I'm ________.
2. I'm ________!
3. ____________________?
4. We're ________.

3 Look and write. How do they look? Use some words from the box.

angry	bored	happy	hungry	sad
scared	surprised	thirsty	tired	

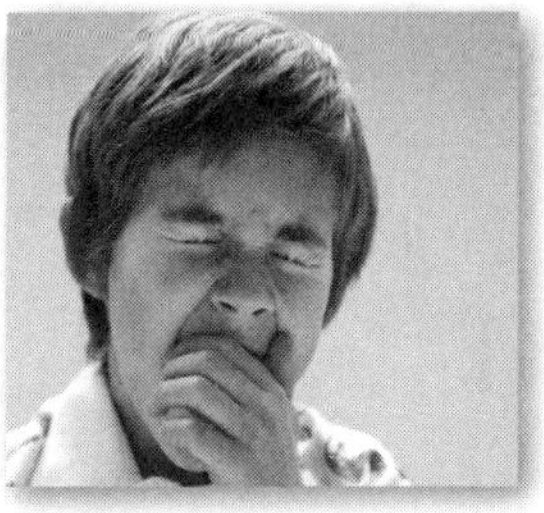

1. ____________________

2. ____________________

3. ____________________

4. ____________________

4 **Read.** Look at the pictures. Match.

a

b

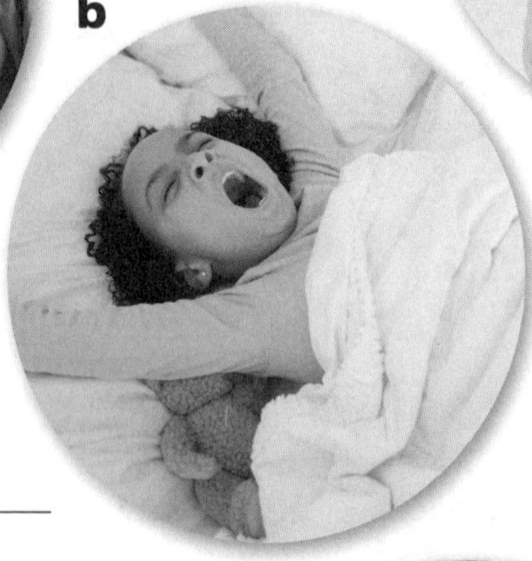

c

d

e

1. He's crying. ______
2. She's laughing. ______
3. He's smiling. ______
4. She's yawning. ______
5. He's frowning. ______

5 **Listen and write.** TR: 46

1. The girl is happy. She's ______________.
2. My sister is ______________. She feels sad.
3. The boy is ______________. He's not happy.
4. It's fun to play with my friends! We are ______________.
5. My brother is tired. He's ______________.

GRAMMAR

shelf	**shelves**	There are three **shelves** above the desk.
tooth	**teeth**	I brush my **teeth** every day.
foot	**feet**	You put socks and shoes on your **feet**.
person	**people**	The **people** are laughing.
child	**children**	Some **children** are reading books.
sheep	**sheep**	Two **sheep** are eating.

6 Read and write.

1. My rabbit has two big ____________. (tooth)
2. There are toys and books on the ________ in my room. (shelf)
3. There are ten ____________ on the train. (person)
4. I like to play tag with my ____________. (friend)

7 Read and write. Find and color.

1. Find two ___gloves___. (glove)
2. Find a dog wearing boots on its ________________. (foot)
3. Find three ________________. (sheep)

8 Find the words. Circle the words.

angry
bored
happy
hungry
scared
sad
surprised
thirsty
tired

t	i	r	e	d	p	z	x	b
h	u	n	g	r	y	m	m	o
i	l	l	r	a	d	r	s	r
r	s	t	y	o	r	e	p	e
s	u	r	p	r	i	s	e	d
t	u	w	v	e	f	b	x	r
y	b	s	a	n	l	l	t	y
z	t	c	n	i	o	m	i	o
b	o	a	g	t	i	y	v	l
p	e	r	r	s	a	d	r	p
s	c	e	y	f	l	a	d	p
a	n	d	o	h	a	p	p	y

9 Read. Draw the faces.

1. crying
2. laughing
3. frowning

10 Listen and read. Can you say these fast? TR: 47

1. Four yawning boys bounce yellow balls.
2. Five frowning frogs fly kites.
3. Six smiling sisters see six sheep.
4. Seven crying children count crayons.

11 **Listen to the song.** Write a new verse. Use some words from the box. **TR: 48**

angry	bored	happy	hungry	scared
sad	surprised	thirsty	tired	

It's OK to be ____________________,

or sometimes to feel ____________________.

It's OK to be ____________________,

or sometimes to feel ____________________.

12 **Listen.** Which words have **i** that sounds like the **i** in t**i**red? Circle the numbers. **TR: 49**

1. 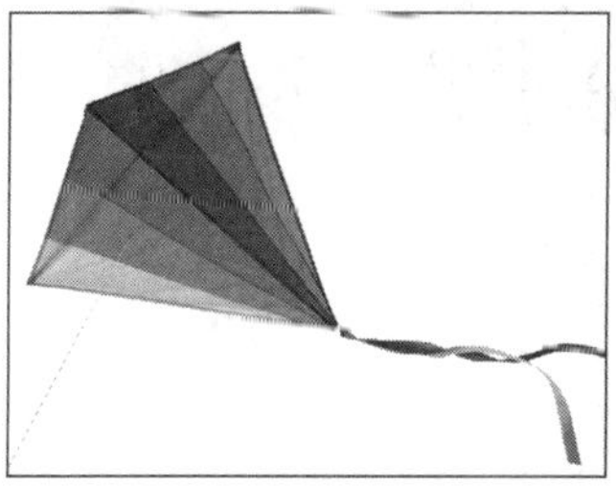

2. 

3. 

4. 

5. 

13 **Say the words.** How many times do you hear **i** as in t**i**red? Write. ☐

climb crying five ride sink smiling surprised writing

14 Listen and read. TR: 50

Clowns

Many people like to watch clowns at the circus. Clowns surprise people. Many people laugh when they watch clowns.

Clowns paint their faces. Some clowns have happy faces. They are always smiling. Some clowns have sad faces. This clown looks sad.

Some people feel scared when they see clowns. What about you?

15 **Read.** Check **T** for *True* or **F** for *False*.

1. Clowns paint their faces. (T) (F)
2. People watch clowns at baseball games. (T) (F)
3. Some clowns have happy faces. (T) (F)

16 **What about you?** Read. Circle. Write.

I like / don't like clowns. Why?

I am ________________________ when I see clowns.

17 Read.

This is a photo of my birthday. I am eight years old. You can see my parents and my friends in this photo. My friends are smiling. They are having fun. I am happy and I am very excited. I have lots of presents! Look at my little sister. She's very happy, too!

18 Write. Choose a photo of you and other people.

1. What special day is it?

____

2. Who are you with?

____

3. How are the people feeling?

____

19 Write. Put your sentences from Activity 18 together.

My special day is ______________________________

____

____

____

____.

Unit 8

Awesome Animals

1 Look and write.

1

2

3

4

5

6

7

8

☐ lion ☐ kangaroo ☐ panda ☐ giraffe

☐ tiger ☐ penguin ☐ hippo ☐ zebra

GRAMMAR

Can a tiger climb a tree?	Yes, it **can.** It **can** climb a tree.	**can't** = cannot
Can a tiger fly?	No, it **can't**. It **can't** fly.	
Can tigers climb trees?	Yes, they **can**. They **can** climb trees.	
Can tigers fly?	No, they **can't**. They **can't** fly.	

2 **Read and match.** Write true sentences. Compare your sentences to a partner's. Are they all true?

A hippo A penguin A panda Lions Zebras Kangaroos	can can't	jump. run. hop. fly. walk. climb.

1. A hippo can't climb.
2. ______________________
3. ______________________
4. ______________________
5. ______________________

3 **What about you?** Write two things you can and can't do.

1. I ______________, but I ______________.
2. I ______________, but I ______________.

4 Which words go together? Circle all the correct letters.

1. long ____________
   a. trunk   b. hair   c. coat   d. apple
2. sharp ____________
   a. jacket   b. claws   c. teeth   d. pencil
3. short ____________
   a. tail   b. ball   c. clock   d. legs
4. colorful ____________
   a. dress   b. crayons   c. feathers   d. kite
5. big ____________
   a. teeth   b. sofa   c. glue   d. ears

5 **Look at the animals.** Write.

1. A penguin has small eyes.
2. ______________________________
3. ______________________________
4. ______________________________
5. ______________________________

GRAMMAR

Does a panda **have** a short tail?	Yes, it **does**.
Does a panda **have** big ears?	No, it **doesn't**.
Do pandas **have** short tails?	Yes, they **do**.
Do pandas **have** big ears?	No, they **don't**.

6 Read and write.

1. Does a kangaroo have big feet?

Yes, it does.

2. ________ a tiger ________________?

________________.

3. ________ a hippo ________________?

________________.

4. ________ penguins ________________?

________________.

5. ________ giraffes ________________?

________________.

7 Listen and answer. Then listen again and write. TR: 51

1. ________________ 3. ________________

2. ________________ 4. ________________

8 **Draw a new animal.** What's its name? What does it have?

9 **Listen and read.** Can you say these fast? **TR: 52**

1. eleven elegant elephants
2. zany zebras zig and zag
3. five fat friendly frogs
4. happy heavy hippos

10 **Listen to the song.** Write a new verse. Use some words from the box. **TR: 53**

A ______________ is an animal

that ______________.

It can't ______________, but it can

______________.

A ______________ is an animal

that ______________.

frog	climb
hippo	crawl
lion	hop
tiger	jump
turtle	run
zebra	swim

11 **Listen.** Which words have **e** that sounds like the **e** in z**e**bra? Draw a line. **TR: 54**

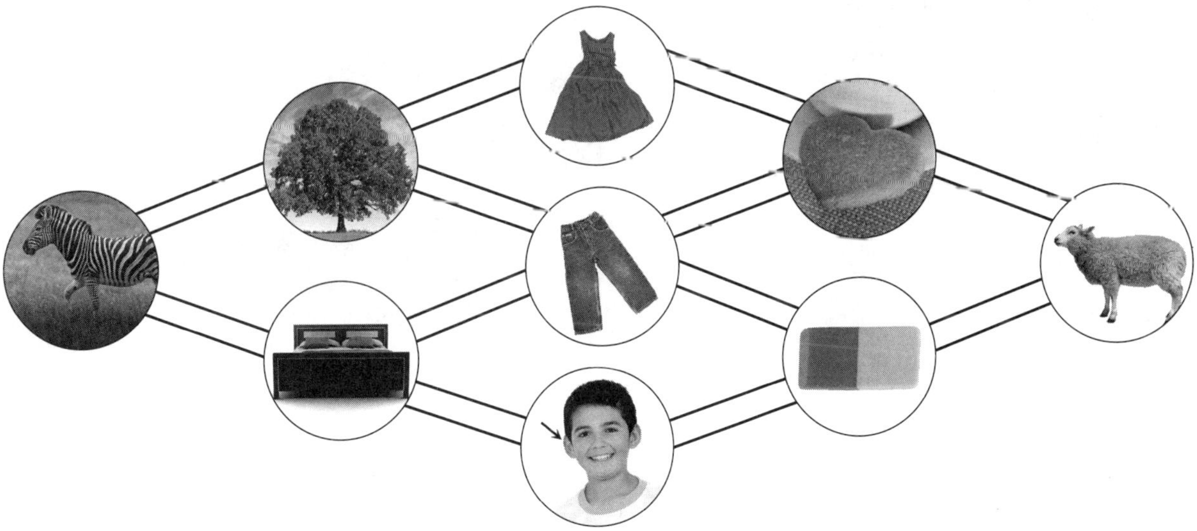

12 **Say the words.** How many times do you hear **e** as in z**e**bra? Write. ☐

eat	evening	green	she
sneakers	tea	teddy bear	teeth

13 Listen and read. TR: 55

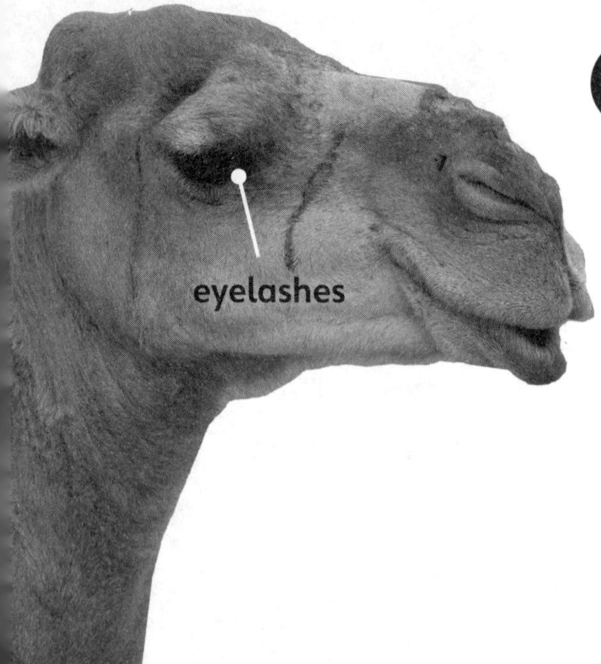

Camels Are Cool!

Camels are awesome animals. They are big and strong and live to be 40 to 50 years old. They live in very, very hot and dry places. Bactrian camels live in rocky deserts in Asia. Arabian camels live in sandy deserts in North Africa.

Bactrian camels have two humps, but Arabian camels have just one hump. All camels can go without food and water for a long time. Their humps help them do this.

Camels have three eyelids on each eye and two sets of long eyelashes, too.

Arabian camel

Bactrian camel

14 Match the sentence parts. Draw lines.

1. Camels live to be
2. Camels live
3. Camels can have
4. Camels have three

a. eyelids on each eye.
b. one or two humps.
c. in very hot and dry places.
d. 40 to 50 years old.

15 **Read.**

My favorite animal is the kangaroo. It is a big animal with a long tail and strong legs. It can hop and jump. It can't walk or run. It has a pocket for a baby kangaroo.

Lisa

16 **Write.** Write about your favorite animal.

1. What is your favorite animal?

____

2. Describe your favorite animal.

____

3. What can your favorite animal do?

____

17 **Write.** Put your sentences from Activity 16 together.

My favorite animal is _______________________________

____

____

____

____

____.

Review

1 **Look.** Read and write. Use words from the boxes.

It's They're

above between next to under

1. Where is the refrigerator?

   It's next to the sink.

2. Where is the bookcase?

   ______ ______ the chairs.

3. Where is the shelf?

   ______ ______ the stove.

4. Where are the chairs?

   ______ ______ the window.

2 **Write.** What is your favorite animal? What does it look like?

______

______

3 **Read.** Look at the pictures. Match.

a

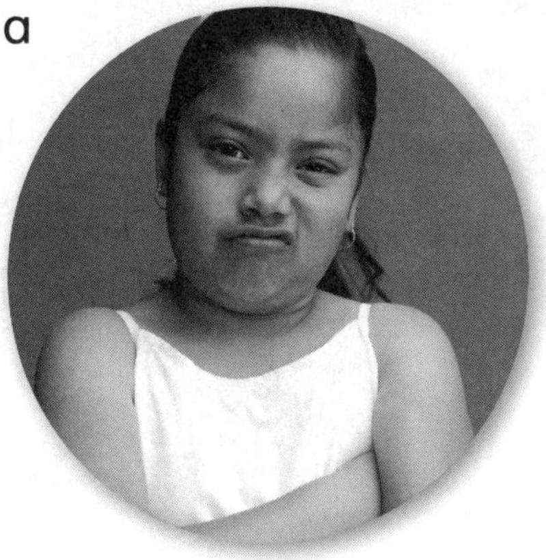

b

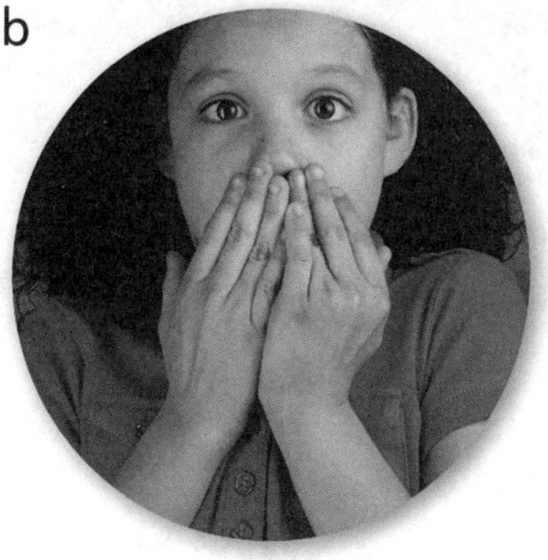

c

1. She looks tired. She's yawning. ____
2. She looks angry. She's frowning. ____
3. She looks surprised. No, she's scared. ____

4 Listen and circle. TR: 56

1. I'm OK.	I'm great!
2. At 8:00.	It's 8:00.
3. When do you eat dinner?	When do you eat lunch?
4. It can hop and jump.	It can fly and swim.
5. A parrot.	A penguin.

5 Read and write.

1. It's 12:00. The ______________ are hungry. (child)
2. Some ______________ go to school at night. (person)
3. Do you like to play ______________? (game)
4. I always brush my ______________ at night. (tooth)

NATIONAL GEOGRAPHIC

EXPLORE OUR WORLD

TR: 57

This is our world.
Everybody's got a song to sing.
Each boy and girl.
This is our world!

I say "our!" You say "world!"
Our!
World!
Our!
World!

I say "boy!" You say "girl!"
Boy!
Girl!
Boy!
Girl!

I say "Everybody move..."
I say "Everybody stop..."
Everybody stop!

This is our world.
Everybody's got a song to sing.
Each boy and girl.
This is our world!

Unit 1

Animals TR: 10

I see animals.
What are they doing?
I see animals.
Can you see them, too?

What do you see?

I see one dog.
Is it running?
Yes, it's running.
It's running in the sun.

What do you see?

I see two cats.
Are they climbing?
Yes, they're climbing.
They're climbing, and it's fun.

Running and climbing,
hopping and singing.
These are things we like to do.

Are you ready?
All together!
Run! Climb! Hop! Sing!

What do you see?

I see three frogs.
Are they hopping?
Yes, they're hopping.
They're hopping on a rock.

What do you see?

I see four birds.
Are they singing?
Yes, they're singing.
They're singing la, la, la!

La lalala!
La lala!

Running and climbing,
hopping and singing.
These are things we like to do.
Are you ready?
All together!
Run! Climb! Hop! Sing!

Unit 2

Our Classroom TR: 17

Reading, writing, talking, listening.
Counting, gluing, cutting, drawing.

What are you doing today?
What are you doing in your classroom?
What are you doing today?
What are you doing in your classroom?

We're cutting. We're gluing.
We're coloring pictures.
We're cutting. We're gluing.
We're coloring pictures.

CHORUS

We're talking. We're writing.
We're listening to our teacher.
We're talking. We're writing.
We're listening to a story.

Reading, writing, talking, listening.
Counting, gluing, cutting, drawing.
Reading, writing, talking, listening.
Counting, gluing, cutting, drawing.
Reading, writing, talking, listening.
Counting, gluing, cutting, drawing.

We're having fun!

What are you doing today?
What are you doing in your classroom?
What are you doing today?
What are you doing in your classroom?

Unit 3

Hot or Cold? TR: 58

Come and look outside.
What do you see?
Today it's snowy.
Put on your boots and coat.
It's cold outside today.

Come and look outside.
What do you see?
Today it's sunny. Put on
your sneakers and shorts.
It's hot outside today.

We dress for the weather.
The weather can be hot or cold.
Sometimes it's hot, sometimes it's cold.
Is it hot or cold today?

Take off your boots and your sweater.
Take off your hat and your coat.
What's the weather like?
Is it hot? Yes!
It's hot outside today.

Put on your boots and your sweater.
Put on your hat and your coat.
What's the weather like?
Is it cold? Yes!
It's cold outside today.

CHORUS

Unit 4

Outside TR: 30

Hey! What do you like to
do outside?

I like to ride a bike.
Yes, I do. Yes, I do.
I like to fly a kite.
Yes, I do. Yes, I do.
I like to play games.
I like to play outside with you.
It's fun, fun, fun!

What is fun for you?
What do you like to do?
Do you like to play?
Let's play outside all day.

What is fun for you?
What do you like to do?
Do you like to play?
Let's play outside all day.
What is fun for you?

Do you like to skateboard?
No, I don't.
Play hide and seek?
No, I don't.
Play basketball?
No. It's boring.

CHORUS

I like to jump rope.
Yes, I do. Yes, I do.
I like to rollerblade.
Yes, I do. Yes, I do.
I like to play soccer.
I like to play with you.
It's fun, fun, fun!

CHORUS

Unit 5

My House TR: 37

Welcome to my house.
This is where I live.
Welcome to my living room.
Is there a place to sit?

The armchair is in front of the fireplace.
Sit down and warm your feet.
The fireplace is next to the bookcase.
Let's find a book to read.

Welcome to my house.
This is where I live.
Welcome to my kitchen.
Is there food in there?

The refrigerator is between the windows.
There's lots of food inside.
Something's cooking on the stove.
May I try some? May I, please?

Welcome to my house.
This is where I live.
Welcome to my bedroom.
Is there a place to sleep?

My pillow is on my bed.
It's where I put my head.
I turn off the light above me.
And then I go to sleep.

Where is the fireplace? It's in the living room.
Where is the stove? It's in the kitchen.
Where is the light? It's in the bedroom.

Welcome to my house.
This is where I live.
It was nice to see you.
Please come again!
Welcome to my house!

Unit 6

Day by Day TR: 42

What time is it? What time is it?
What time is it? Can you tell me?

It's seven o'clock. It's seven o'clock.
It's seven o'clock in the morning.
I always get up at seven o'clock.
I get up at seven every day.

CHORUS

It's eight o'clock. It's eight o'clock.
It's eight o'clock in the morning.
I go to school at eight o'clock.
I always go to school at eight.

CHORUS

It's three o'clock. It's three o'clock.
It's three o'clock in the afternoon.
I always play with friends at three o'clock.
I play with my friends every day.

CHORUS

It's nine o'clock. It's nine o'clock.
It's nine o'clock at night.
I go to sleep at nine o'clock.
I go to sleep at nine every day.

Unit 7

Emotions TR: 48

Sometimes I'm happy.
Sometimes I'm surprised.
Sometimes I'm just silly.
I'm laughing inside!

Sometimes I'm angry.
Sometimes I'm just bored.
Sometimes I'm excited.

How are you?
How do you feel?
How are you?
Tell me, please. How do you feel?

Sometimes I'm smiling.
I'm laughing at a joke!

Sometimes I'm crying.
I feel sad.

Sometimes I'm tired.
Sometimes I'm worried.
Sometimes I'm feeling scared.

It's OK to be happy,
or sometimes to feel sad.
It's OK to be silly,
or sometimes to feel mad.

CHORUS
CHORUS

Unit 8

Awesome Animals TR: 53

A parrot is a bird that flies.
It can't swim, but it can fly.
A parrot is a bird that flies
high in the sky.

A monkey swings from tree to tree,
tree to tree, tree to tree.
A monkey swings from tree to tree.
Why can't we?

I want to be a monkey in a tree!
I want to fly high up in the sky!

A penguin is a bird that swims.
It can't fly, but it can swim.
A penguin is a bird that swims
deep in the sea.

A kangaroo can hop and jump.
It can't climb, but it can jump.
A kangaroo can hop and jump
just like me.

I want to be a monkey in a tree!
And I want to fly high up in the sky!
I want to be a monkey in a tree!
And I want to fly high up in the sky!